Celebrating Mothers Around the World

Brief Poetic Insights

by O.K. FATAI

Published by OK Publishing

Wellington, New Zealand

Email: OK.Publishingnz@gmail.com

Full catalogue in print data may be obtained from the National Library of New Zealand

ISBN-13: 978-0-473-51137-1

Dedication

To all those who treasure the immeasurable value of mothers and to all mothers around the world who work\ tirelessly for their family and others.

CONTENTS

Acknowledgements

I appreciate the help of my family and friends who value the place and roles that mothers play in their life journey.

we look up to

we look up to the shining light
that shines brightly, with eyes that give everyone great delights

rising beauty; she deserves
deep respect, people's shining love, to her serve

stories of courage and her inner strength;
both tell the silent voices that applaud her at length

she is within reach, even with the beauty of the stars in her eyes
if she is voted on beauty, everyone will all say ayes;

her spirit recognizes the journey
her huge love for family, friends and humanity

she experienced respect so deeply
she appear as the unique stand out one, rising steeply

the world so much in awe
and marvel in their spirits still raw

in a journey filled with the responsibilities of life
her life is now a respectable decision maker

and her strength to cope with pressures
on a journey we all treasure.

goes from strength

it takes inner strength
to do what she can do at length
as she goes from strength to strength

it takes inner courage
to be someone that encourages
people to stand up and not discourage

it takes inner resolves
to let herself be involved
in so many roles that continue to evolve
despite the constant changes
she is always there
fulfilling responsibilities
giving service with a heart so divine

true to the values

true to the values people behold
she is the one with touches of gold;
thanks to her, her children are now more bold
to pursue their dreams just like she did,
we giggled as we are just like dreaming kids
and we see her as the idol with the smiles,
angels even stop to see her beauty styles

true to the desires of people's hearts
the voice that sounds very smart
and the life that is on top of the chart
we giggled as we are like dreaming kids
with hopes, just like her, that may not be hidden
there goes the angels smiling at her, no kidding

so many...

so many admire what she can do
she is really the one in the who's who
of so many things, we can only say hey yahoo!

so many look up to her
what title should we use to refer to her?
to a beauty queen that people prefer
to be called as one of their own

so many have made decisions
to watch her moves to see her precision
so many loved the messages she had given us
one - that if she can do it, we can also do it.

the path

some of her friends like to follow the path to stardom
because they see her as like a kingdom
with one of a kind star - that's her!

some of her friends like follow the path to love
because they see her as like the heavenly dove
that signals peace and quietness
in a world that is full of disquiet

some of her friends like to follow the path to connections
as they love her many loving and connected stories
for even hills line up the ways
mountains bow down on the streets
as they respect a lady so sweet.

so deeply

we are getting so deeply in wonders
with a life that had corrected many blunders
and become rainbows to so many thunders

we are getting so deeply in wonders
how can we feel so under
for her smiles can lift us up to beyond-ers

we are getting so deeply in wonders
we are crossing the river of amazement
and drink from the water that is crystal clear
thanks so much to her life with many wonders.

visit

a young girl visited her granddad at hospital.
the young girl gave her granddad a hug and said,
"grandpa i want to be a superstar like mum.
is that possible?"

the grandad looked at her grand daughter
and with a smile said, "you know, i have star like qualities in my
heart.
i have the courage to face challenges
i am contented and i am free."

the granddaughter paused for a while and then replied,
"but is that the way to become a superstar?"

the granddad smiled again then said,
"you are already a superstar! it's because you give so much love
away as you've done today."

the young girl smiled and replied,
"i wish i can have the heart of a superstar to start with granddad."

the granddad sat up and said,
"you've already got it. every time you are showing love to your
family, you have the hearts of superstar."

the young girl smiled and gave her granddad another hug,
a hug of a superstar, and said, "i now know how to begin to be a
superstar like mum."

it's here

to have love it's here
it's right here

to have courage it's here
it's right here

to have fame it's here
it's right here

to have a shining life it's here
it's right here

to have a future that looks bright it's here
it's right here

just look here, into her heart
just look here, into her dreams
just look here, into her perseverance
just look here, into her courage
they are the qualities she has
and you can have them too.

beauty sometimes...

beauty sometimes is
    to keep on doing
      despite challenges

beauty sometimes is to
    keep on going
      despite barriers

beauty sometimes is
    to continue battling
      despite all the odds

beauty sometimes is
    to decide to do it
      again despite failings

beauty sometimes is
    to look back and
      decide to continue forward

sometimes that is beauty...

turn open the photo album!
let me see that woman on the front page!
i can see unending beauties inside her heart!

like a step

beauty is like a step
that leads to a heaven of love

beauty is like a step
that leads to a spirit that shines

beauty is like a step
that leads to a life that attracts

beauty is like a step
that leads to lives that set examples

beauty is like a step
that begs the world to love one another

are we beauties like her?

every day

every day we live lives that are influenced
by family and friends
by the media and society

every day we think of actions to accomplish
and dreams to pursue
and destiny to reach

every day we live lives influenced
by colleagues and organizations
by beliefs and values

her every day is somewhat like our every day,
occupied with normal every day tasks and roles,
like work and family, receiving and giving love;
thanks to how she spend her every day
she is a blessing to so many others every day.

beauty does not...

beauty does not
reveal itself in arrogance

beauty does not
reveal itself in fires of anger

beauty does not
reveal itself in acts of hatred

beauty does not
dwell on the mistakes of the past

for beauty is
something that is inside us

that's why she has so many admiring friends
she also has so much beauties on the inside.

inner beauty

inner beauty is as much about
    inward feelings and outward actions

it takes inner beauty
    to maintain inner freedoms and values

it takes inner beauty
    to take the heart to new frontiers

it takes inner beauty
    to realize what is truly in the soul

it takes inner beauty
    to smile despite challenges

it takes inner beauty
    to have the inner resolve to love others

we are proud to be her friends
    as she has so many inner beauties.

to be famous

to be famous doesn't
    have to be
    huge bold actions

to be famous doesn't
    have to be
    always fearless decisions

to be famous doesn't
    have to be
    the desire to face huge challenges

to be famous doesn't
    have to be the
    decision to always move forward

you can be famous if you make
    day to day decision to
    live from moment to moment

you can be famous if you do
    the actions of smiling
    to a complete stranger

you can be famous if you have
    the desire to
    give just a little help

when you do those actions
you will be famous to the divine

and when we think of it
what really matter is when we
are famous to the divine
just like her
yes, just like her.

she reaches out...

to her colleagues she is a person
who reaches out to them with the graces of her smiles

to her family she is a person
who reveals her life right on daily, in their laughter and cries

to her friends she is a person
who decides to live her dreams
and help the wishes of so many others

to her relatives she is a person
who have lots of courage
and inner beauties like living waters

to her country she is a person
whose outer beauty is without compare

to her nation she is a person
whose inner beauty shines like a morning star

she reaches out
yes, she reaches out.

we must not be...

we must not be over proud
when we see the lives she blessed
for even her gaze and smiles
can lift a mood out of the valleys
but be encouraged
as there are beauties in people
there is inner and outer beauties in people
there is humility in people
and abundance of grace in people
and to be real we all
have imperfections in our actions
but let's be thankful as well
that we have someone to behold
and invite her smiles and sweetness
to our own lounge and homes
let's be thankful and be grateful
that the divine gifted her to all of her
family and friends.

journey with...

journey with choices
the many alternatives
of faces and beauties
that we daily admire
right in front on tvs,
and behold our attentions
on radios and magazines;

journey with choices
the many alternatives
of people to learn from;
and examples to follow
and sometimes entertained
us in ways beyond imaginations;

journey with choices
her family had made their choices
it's her wonderment and amazement
that steals the imaginations of so many;
her family had made their choices
she is the one they prefer to treasure forever.

the wonders of the world

amazing wonders
filled our experiences

on a daily basis
there are amazing wonders

of being alive
and amazing wonders

of having friends and family
amazing wonders of nature

and the beauties of
the environment

also the beauties of
man-made structures

but there is also
amazing wonders in

that someone who has
outer and inner beauties

she is an example of beauties of all sorts
and so many other roles to fulfill;

she is an amazing mother
to such lovely kids and family;

she is simply one of a kind
one of the amazing
wonders of the world,
her family would add.

wings

spread your wings
and fly above the sky;

learn from her
and have the courage to spread

your wings and fly.
everyone will see you

up above and will
have the desires

to fly higher and higher
for when she sets examples to the world

be courageous in your actions
people will see your inner

qualities and will follow
the light you had shone

for her qualities
had spread far and wide

after each day, she let you off
to spread your wings and start

to fly and fly
higher and higher.

every day

every day we see someone
working in people's lives

every day we see someone
who lights up someone's day

every day we see someone
whose smiles touches a hungry soul

every day we see someone
who lift up a spirit with acts of kindness

when we get to see her more and more
we will realize she is an angel for our every days.

bigger and bigger

her fame is getting bigger
her shining face is right up on top,
her smiles that steal hearts are
there always on our hearts,
her star like qualities is getting bigger;

but her soul remains family loving
her spirit remains firmly grounded
her mind remains humble and firmly
grounded in her family and up bringing;

we can only wonder what would happen
if we are on her shoes and how can we can cope
with so much shining from her life,

we can only look at her and follow
the examples she has set
and remains firmly grounded
remains firmly rooted.

one more way

there is another way
to let love flows like a river

there is another way
to let your actions shine

there is another way
to let your smiles bless another

there is another way
to let peace spread inside us

there is another way
to let your life be a blessing

it is one more way
it is *your way*

but let me add, just let
a loving mother's way be your way

and things will be simple
and easily completed.

matter of choosing

prestige and fame is
sometimes a decision
to be brave because of
all the media frenzy

prestige and fame
is sometimes about
choosing right,
whenever the situation arises,
it's about choosing to be

courageous and humble
to be loving and caring;

prestige and fame
is really a matter for the heart
to decide that prestige and fame
will not really change
what is really in the soul
just like what she had shown to the world.

miracles

we hear stories of extra-ordinary
things that a person has done

we hear stories of amazing feats
a person had accomplished

and from time to time we hear
stories of miracles. often miracles

are a domain for the divine and religion
but those who know a loving mother, when they

see her love for her family and the little
children that grows and bless her days,

the world can easily conclude
that she is a divine miracle
that touches their hearts deeply.

what is

what is in your heart?
    what is in your soul?
        what is in your spirit?
is it amazement?
    is it a dream?
        is it vision?

is it people or community?
    when we delve deeply into what's
    in our hearts, it takes courage

to face what is in our hearts
    and also to be true to what
    is in our souls

thanks to a mother like her
    who faces her heart and souls
    and be true to what is really hers.

Other books by O.K. Fatai

1. Poems on Values to Succeed Worldwide in Life: Being Responsible
2. Poems on Values to Succeed Worldwide in Life: Courage
3. Poems on Values to Succeed Worldwide in Life: Good Families
4. Poems on Values to Succeed Worldwide in Life: Forgiveness
5. Poems on Values to Succeed Worldwide in Life: Good Friends
6. Poems on Values to Succeed Worldwide in Life: Grace
7. Poems on Values to Succeed Worldwide in Life: Hope
8. Poems on Values to Succeed Worldwide in Life: Humility
9. Poems on Values to Succeed Worldwide in Life: Joy
10. Poems on Values to Succeed Worldwide in Life: Justice
11. Poems on Values to Succeed Worldwide in Life: Life
12. Poems on Values to Succeed Worldwide in Life: Love
13. Poems on Values to Succeed Worldwide in Life: Mercy
14. Poems on Values to Succeed Worldwide in Life: Peace
15. Poems on Values to Succeed Worldwide in Life: Perseverance
16. Poems on Values to Succeed Worldwide in Life: Faith
17. Poems on Values to Succeed Worldwide in Life: Harmony with Nature
18. Poems on Values to Succeed Worldwide in Life: Education

More books by O.K. Fatai

1. Poems on Values to Succeed Worldwide in Life: Understanding and Wisdom
2. Poems on Values to Succeed Worldwide in Life: Work and Optimism
3. Poems on Values to Succeed Worldwide in Life: Adversity and Confidence
4. Poems on Values to Succeed Worldwide in Life: Listening and Diversity and Unity
5. Poems on Values to Succeed Worldwide in Life: Sharing and Honesty
6. Poems on Values to Succeed Worldwide in Life: Simplicity and Harmony
7. Poems on Values to Succeed Worldwide in Life: Unity in Diversity and Connections
8. Poems on Values to Succeed Worldwide in Life: Contentment and Acceptance
9. Poems on Values to Succeed Worldwide in Life: Excellence and Compassion
10. Poems on Values to Succeed Worldwide in Life: Generosity and Being Passionate
11. Poems on Values to Succeed Worldwide in Life: Gentleness and Trustworthy
12. Poems on Values to Succeed Worldwide in Life: Patience and Being Tactful
13. Poems on Values to Succeed Worldwide in Life: Purity and Integrity
14. Poems on Values to Succeed Worldwide in Life: Being Modest and Persistence
15. Poems on Values to Succeed Worldwide in Life: Respect and Loyalty

About the Author

O.K. Fatai is a poet and author from Wellington, New Zealand. He likes to spend time writing poems, especially ones that explore the different aspects of values and virtues that are widely accepted in different cultures today.

O.K. Fatai enjoys writing songs and some of his forthcoming books are song lyrics that look at different values and virtues and some of their appeal to us today. In his spare time, he writes short stories and novels. He is looking forward to sharing these stories with readers around the world, and he has already published some short stories and has more than ten forthcoming publications in children's literature. O.K. Fatai is writing novels for young adults and adults. He is also a playwright and has written and/or directed more than eight short plays.

He likes painting abstract art and enjoys the different interpretations of abstract paintings, especially when they reflect values and virtues. He is a photographer who likes to take photographs of nature and the environment, which has a special place in his heart. He is keen on filming and editing videos, plays musical instruments and is part of a local band.

O.K. Fatai is a volunteer at the United Nations and regional prisons in Wellington and, for many years has volunteered to more than ten other organizations. He works in the health sector and is a consultant for three different online companies, and the President and CEO of more than three businesses. He is also available as an external consultant to the United Nations, the European Bank for Reconstruction and Development, and the Asian Development Bank.